for
Margot
and
Iggy

An Apple
and
An Adventure

by Martin Cendreda

AN APPLE AND AN ADVENTURE, June 2017. Published by Archaia, a division of Boom Entertainment, Inc. An Apple and an Adventure is ™ & © 2017 Martin Cendreda. All Rights Reserved. Archaia™ and the Archaia logo are trademarks of Boom Entertainment, Inc., registered in various countries and categories. All characters, events, and institutions depicted herein are fictional. Any similarity between any of the names, characters, persons, events, and/or institutions in this publication to actual names, characters, and persons, whether living or dead, events, and/or institutions is unintended and purely coincidental.

SIERRA HAHN Editor SOPHIE PHILIPS-ROBERTS Assistant Editor

BOOM! Studios
5670 Wilshire Boulevard, Suite 450
Los Angeles, CA 90036-5679.
Printed in China. First Printing.

ISBN: 978-1-68415-064-9, eISBN: 978-1-61398-741-4

ARCHAIA.

Pictures and words by
Martin Cendreda

Avast! An apple and an adventure...

Buddies bathing by a bronto.

Cute critters crouching on a crystal.

Drawing dinos in the dark.

Eek! An electric eel egg!

Feathered friend fetched a fish.

A gang of galloping goliaths.

Honking hoppers hiding from the heat.

Inside an igloo, on an island of ice.

Just a jaunty little jungle jam.

Kraken keeps keys in the kelp.

Lots of leaves for lunch.

Making mudpies by moonlight.

Nine newts napping at night.

Observing the obsidian objects.

Petting a pack of petite plesiosaurs.

A quarrelsome quartet, on a quest.

Rusty robot reclines by the river.

Slip-sliding down stripey sauropods.

Tiny T-rex topples trees.

Uh-oh! Upside-down underwater...

Various velociraptors veiled in vines.

Wooly wanders through the
wet and windy white.

"X" marks the spot exactly!

Yapping yelpers eating yummy yams.

Catching "ZZZZ's" in the zebra zone.